Algebra Readiness

by Sarah Jane Brian

SCHOLASTIC
PROFESSIONAL BOOKS

New York ✳ Toronto ✳ London ✳ Auckland ✳ Sydney

$5y \leq 3y + 10$ ✳ $6(x + 3) = 6x + 18$ ✳ $3x + 2y = 24$ ✳ $x^2 = 25$ ✳ $4c + 6 + 3c < 50$

Edited by Sarah Glasscock

Cover design by Jaime Lucero

Cover illustration by Michael Moran

Interior design by Ellen Matlach Hassell
for Boultinghouse & Boultinghouse, Inc.

Interior illustrations by Michael Moran and Manuel Rivera

ISBN 0-590-37369-2

Contents

(continued on the next page)

☀ Activity includes a student reproducible.

✳ Activity includes a student reproducible.

Introduction

With this book of activities, part of a six-book mathematics series, we hope to make teaching and understanding algebra fun, creative, and exciting.

An Overview of the Book

Table of Contents

The table of contents features the activity names and page numbers, as well as stars to mark student reproducibles. Activities are categorized by algebra topic, so you may use the table of contents as a scope and sequence.

Teaching Pages

Everything you need to know is on the teaching page, but you also have the option of tailoring the activities to meet students' individual needs and to address the wide variety of skills displayed in your classroom.

Learning Logo

A logo indicating the algebra topic being discussed appears at the top of the page. The logo is correlated to the topics in the table of contents. This will enable you to key the activities to your mathematics curriculum quickly and easily.

Learning Objective

The objective clearly states the primary aim of the activity.

Grouping

This indicates whether the whole class, individual students, pairs, or cooperative groups should perform the task. If an activity lends itself to more than one grouping, the choices are indicated. Again, if you feel that another grouping is more appropriate to your classroom, feel free to alter the activity accordingly.

Materials

To cut your preparation time, all materials necessary for the main activity (including student reproducible) and its extension are listed. Most of the materials are probably already in your classroom. If an activity has a student reproducible with it, the page number of the reproducible is listed here.

Advance Preparation

A few activities require some minimal advance preparation on your part. All the directions you need are given here. You may also choose to let students take over some or all of the preparation.

Directions

The directions usually begin with suggestions on how to introduce or review the algebra topic, including any terms and/or formulas. Step-by-step details on how to do the activity follow. When pertinent, specific strategies that might help students in solving problems are suggested.

Taking It Farther

This section on the teaching page offers suggestions on how you can extend and enrich the activity. Students who require extra help and those who need a challenge will both benefit when you move the activity to a different level.

Assessing Skills

The key questions and/or common errors pointed out in this section will help alert you to students' progress. (In fact, you may want to jot down more questions on the page.) Use the information you gather about students here in conjunction with the teacher assessment form that appears on page 63 of the book.

Answers

When answers are called for, they appear on the teaching page.

Student Reproducibles

- About one-third of the activities have a companion student reproducible page for you to duplicate and distribute. These activities are marked with a star in the table of contents.

Do I Have Problems!

These two pages are filled with fun and challenging Problems of the Day that you may write on the board or post on the bulletin board. The answers appear in brackets at the end of each problem.

Assessment

Student Self-Evaluation Form

At the end of the activity, hand out these forms for students to complete. Emphasize that their responses are for themselves as well as you. Evaluating their own performances will help students clarify their thinking and understand more about their reasoning.

Teacher Assessment Form and Scoring Rubric

The sign of a student's success with an activity is more than a correct answer. As the NCTM stresses, problem solving, communication, reasoning, and connections are equally important in the mathematical process. How a student arrives at the answer—the strategies she or he uses or discards, for instance—can be as important as the answer itself. This assessment form and scoring rubric will help you determine the full range of students' mastery of skills.

$$5y \leq 3y + 10 \quad * \quad 6(x + 3) = 6x + 18 \quad * \quad 3x + 2y = 24 \quad * \quad x^2 = 25 \quad * \quad 4c + 6 + 3c < 50$$

National Council of Teachers of Mathematics Standards

The activities in this book, and the rest of the series, have been written with the National Council of Teachers of Mathematics (NCTM) Standards in mind. The first four standards—Mathematics as Problem Solving, Mathematics as Communication, Mathematics as Reasoning, and Mathematical Connections—form the philosophical underpinning of the activities.

Standard 1: Mathematics as Problem Solving
The open-ended structure of the activities, and their extension, builds and strengthens students' problem-solving skills.

Standard 2: Mathematics as Communication
Class discussion at the beginning and ending of the activities is an integral part of these activities.

Additionally, communication is fostered when students work in pairs or cooperative groups and when individuals share and compare work.

Standard 3: Mathematics as Reasoning
Communicating their processes in working these activities gives students the opportunity to understand and appreciate their own thinking.

Standard 4: Mathematical Connections
A variety of situations has been incorporated into the activities to give students a broad base on which to apply mathematics. Topics range from real-life experiences (historical and contemporary) to the whimsical and fantastic, so students can expand their mathematical thinking to include other subject areas.

More specifically, the activities in this book address the following NCTM Standards.

Grades 5–8

Standard 5: Number and Number Relationships
* Understand, represent, and use numbers in a variety of equivalent forms (integer, fraction, decimal, percent, exponential, and scientific notation) in real-world and mathematical problem situations.
* Develop number sense for whole numbers, fractions, decimals, integers, and rational numbers.

Standard 6: Number Systems and Number Theory
* Develop and order relations for whole numbers, fractions, decimals, integers, and rational numbers.
* Understand how the basic arithmetic operations are related to each other.
* Develop and apply number theory concepts (e.g., primes, factors, and multiples) in real-world and mathematical problem situations.

Standard 7: Computation and Estimation
* Compute with whole numbers, fractions, decimals, integers, and rational numbers.
* Develop, analyze, and explain procedures for computation and techniques for estimation.
* Select and use an appropriate method for computing from among mental arithmetic, paper-and-pencil, calculator, and computer methods.
* Use computation, estimation, and proportions to solve problems.

Standard 8: Patterns and Functions
* Describe, extend, analyze, and create a wide variety of patterns.
* Describe and represent relationships with tables, graphs, and rules.
* Analyze functional relationships to explain how a change in one quantity results in a change in another.
* Use patterns and functions to represent and solve problems.

Standard 8: Algebra
* Understand the concepts of variable, expression, and equation.
* Represent situations and number patterns with tables, graphs, verbal rules, and equations and explore the interrelationships of representations.
* Analyze tables and graphs to identify properties and relationships.
* Develop confidence in solving linear equations using concrete, informal, and formal methods.
* Investigate inequalities and nonlinear equations informally.
* Apply algebraic methods to solve a variety of real-world and mathematical problems.

Tasty Properties

Students get a flavorful look at U.S. cities named after foods as they find out about the properties of addition and multiplication.

⟳→ Directions

1. Duplicate the *Tasty Properties* reproducible.
2. Review the properties of addition and multiplication. Write the following definitions and examples on the board and discuss them with the class.

Commutative Properties

Addition: You can change the order of addends without changing the sum. EXAMPLE: $8 + 3 = 11$, $3 + 8 = 11$, $8 + 3 = 3 + 8$

Multiplication: You can change the order of factors without changing the product. EXAMPLE: $7 \times 5 = 35$, $5 \times 7 = 35$, $7 \times 5 = 5 \times 7$

Associative Properties

Addition: You can change the way addends are grouped without changing the sum. EXAMPLE: $7 + (12 + 3) = 22$, $(7 + 12) + 3 = 22$, $7 + (12 + 3) = (7 + 12) + 3$

Multiplication: You can change the way factors are grouped without changing the product. EXAMPLE: $(9 \times 5) \times 8 = 360$, $5 \times (9 \times 8) = 360$, $(9 \times 5) \times 8 = 5 \times (9 \times 8)$

Identity Properties

Addition: The sum of any addend and zero is the addend. EXAMPLE: $2 + 0 = 2$

Multiplication: The product of any factor and 1 is the factor. EXAMPLE: $6 \times 1 = 6$

☆ Taking It Farther

✳ Ask students to explain whether subtraction is commutative. Also query them about whether subtraction is associative.

✳ Have students look up the words *commute, associate,* and *identity* in the dictionary. How do the words relate to the properties of addition and multiplication?

✓ Assessing Skills

A common error is always to identify a property as associative if there are more than two numbers. Check to see if students can correctly identify cases of the commutative property that use three or more numbers.

LEARNING OBJECTIVE

Students use and identify the Commutative, Associative, and Identity Properties of addition and multiplication.

GROUPING

Individual

MATERIALS

✳ *Tasty Properties* reproducible (p. 9)

ANSWERS

2. 5 Vermont, Identity property of addition

3. 15×4 Montana, Commutative property of multiplication

4. $8 + (3 + 7)$ Florida, Associative property of addition

5. $(x + 4)$ Iowa, Identity property of multiplication

6. $y12x$ California, Commutative property of multiplication

7. $5 + v$, Pennsylvania, Commutative property of addition

8. cd Mississippi, Identity property of addition

9. $j + 11$ Illinois, Associative property of addition

Tasty Properties

How would you like to own property in Cookietown, Oklahoma? All across the United States, you can find cities named after food. To find out where the mouthwatering towns below are located, use the commutative, associative, and identity properties of addition and multiplication.

For each problem, circle the statement that completes the equation correctly. Next to it is the state where the town is located. Write the state. Then write the property you used to find the answer. The first one is done for you.

1. Noodle, _Texas_____ $(4 \times 2) \times 3 = ?$ $2(4 + 3)$ Idaho   ⟨$2(4 \cdot 3)$ Texas⟩

   What property is shown? _Associative property of multiplication_____

2. Beanville, _____ $5 \cdot 0 = ?$ 5×0 Hawaii   5 Vermont

   What property is shown? _____

3. Olive, _____ $4 \times 15 = ?$ 15×4 Montana 14×5 Washington

   What property is shown? _____

4. Spuds, _____ $7 + (8 + 3) = ?$ $(7 + 8)3$ Michigan $8 + (3 + 7)$ Florida

   What property is shown? _____

5. Walnut, _____ $(x + 4) \times 1 = ?$ $4x$ New York $(x + 4)$ Iowa

   What property is shown? _____

6. Jelly, _____ $12xy = ?$ $y12x$ California $24y$ North Carolina

   What property is shown? _____

7. Mustard, _____ $v + 5 = ?$ $5v$ Colorado $5 + v$ Pennsylvania

   What property is shown? _____

8. Eggville, _____ $cd + 0 = ?$ cd Mississippi $c + d$ Delaware

   What property is shown? _____

9. Sandwich, _____ $(7 + j) + 4 = ?$ $(j \cdot 11)$ Georgia $j + 11$ Illinois

   What property is shown? _____

Opposites Subtract

And sometimes, opposites add, multiply, or divide! Students learn about inverse operations by finding inverses to actions from their daily lives.

⟳→ Directions

1. Remind students that inverse operations are operations that "undo" each other.

2. Write the following statements on the board:

   a. $17 + 5 = 22$ **b.** $11 - 7 = 4$ **c.** $6 \cdot 2 = 12$ **d.** $15 \div 5 = 3$

   Have students "undo" the math by using inverse operations. Call on volunteers to share their answers.

3. Write the following list of everyday actions on the board:

   a. gaining 10 yards in football
   b. taking 3 steps backward
   c. withdrawing $20 from a bank account
   d. breaking a plate into 5 equal pieces

   Ask students to give an example of an inverse of each action.

4. Challenge students to find the math operations that were done and then undone by their inverses in each example.

5. Direct pairs to come up with their own lists of inverses for real-life actions. One student writes an action on a sheet of paper, and the other student supplies the inverse action. Then partners switch roles. They continue until they have at least five examples of actions and inverses.

★ Taking It Farther

Do the following example on the board to show that inverse operations can be used to solve equations:

$$n \div 4 = 7$$
$$n = 7 \times 4$$
$$n = 28$$

Let students use inverse operations to solve equations such as:

$$r - 12 = 14 \qquad k \cdot 3 = 27 \qquad h + 7 = 25 \qquad x \div 6 = 4$$

✔ Assessing Skills

* When solving problems, students may use the operation in the problem instead of its inverse.

* Also note whether students check their answers using estimation or by plugging the variable value into the original equation.

Olympic Flips

As they practice finding reciprocals, students will flip for this fun maze!

Directions

1. Duplicate the *Olympic Flips* reproducible.

2. Review the term *reciprocal* or *multiplicative inverse.* Remind students that if they multiply a number by its reciprocal, the product is always 1. One way to find a reciprocal is to write the number as a fraction and switch the numerator and the denominator. Write the following examples on the board:

$$\frac{1}{3} \times \frac{3}{1} = 1$$

$$\frac{4}{7} \times \frac{7}{4} = 1$$

$$\frac{a}{b} \bullet \frac{b}{a} = 1$$

3. Note that a mixed number must be changed to a fraction before finding the reciprocal. Explain, too, that reciprocals may be written in lowest terms. Write the following examples on the board:

What is the reciprocal of $5\frac{2}{3}$? $$5\frac{2}{3} = \frac{17}{3}$$ $$\frac{17}{3} \times \frac{3}{17} = 1$$ The reciprocal is $\frac{3}{17}$.	What is the reciprocal of $\frac{4}{9}$? $$\frac{4}{9} \times \frac{9}{4} = 1$$ $$\frac{9}{4} = 2\frac{1}{4}$$ The reciprocal of $\frac{4}{9}$ is $2\frac{1}{4}$.

4. Have students complete the reproducible on their own.

☆ Taking It Farther

Encourage students to calculate the reciprocals for numbers in the maze that were not part of the path to the finish line.

✓ Assessing Skills

✳ Observe whether students make the error of inverting just the fractional part of a mixed number, leaving the whole number alone.

✳ Note whether students check their work by multiplying the number and its reciprocal.

LEARNING OBJECTIVE

Students find the reciprocals of integers, fractions, and mixed numbers.

GROUPING

Individual

MATERIALS

✳ *Olympic Flips* reproducible (p. 12)

ANSWERS

$\frac{14}{9}$ $\frac{9}{14}$, $\frac{2}{3}$ $1\frac{1}{2}$, $\frac{1}{6}$ 6, $-\frac{4}{5}$ $-\frac{5}{4}$, $2\frac{1}{8}$ $\frac{8}{17}$, $\frac{32}{2}$ $\frac{1}{16}$, $\frac{2}{20}$ 10

11

Olympic Flips

Help gymnast Airy Shrugg flip across the mat and score a perfect **10**!

Begin at Start. Find the reciprocal of $\frac{14}{9}$. The reciprocal will always be in the top circle of a pair of circles. Trace the line to that circle. Then find the reciprocal of the fraction in the bottom circle. Trace a line to the circle with its reciprocal. You can move in any direction, as long as the circles are connected by a line. Keep moving until you reach Finish.

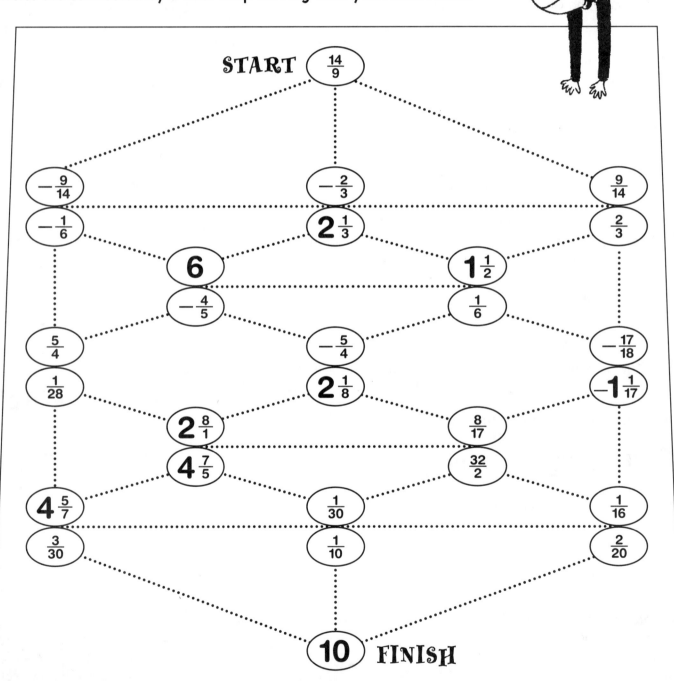

Algebra Readiness Scholastic Professional Books

Have No Fear

Does your class suffer from algebraphobia? Students practice using the distributive property and learn about some common phobias.

➔ Directions

1. Duplicate a copy of the *Have No Fear* reproducible for each student.

2. Review the distributive property with students. You may want to write the following definition on the board:

   For any numbers *x*, *y*, and *z*, $x(y + z) = xy + xz$.

3. Write the following expressions on the board. Have volunteers use the distributive property to rewrite the expressions. (Answers are given in brackets.) Note: Students should not compute the value of the expression.

$4(3 + 7)$	$[4 \bullet 3 + 4 \bullet 7]$
$5k + 5y$	$[5(k + y)]$
$6(x + 3)$	$[6x + 18]$

4. Explain to students that an expression in simplest form should have no like terms and no parentheses. Ask: *Which expressions written on the board are in simplest form?* [the last expression]

5. Finally, have students complete the reproducible on their own. Note that in some cases they will have to use other properties, such as the commutative property of addition, as well as the distributive property.

✪ Taking It Farther

Have students use properties to rewrite each expression in the activity in as many ways as they can. For example, $4(x + 3)$ can also be written as $2(2x + 6)$, $4x + 12$, $(x + 3)4$, or $2x \bullet 2 + 12$.

✔ Assessing Skills

Observe whether students are completing the distribution. For example, some students may rewrite $8(4 + 6)$ as $32 + 6$, instead of as $32 + 48$.

LEARNING OBJECTIVE

Students use the distributive property.

GROUPING

Individual

MATERIALS

✳ *Have No Fear* reproducible (p. 14)

ANSWERS

2. $4x$, Fear of Darkness

3. $8p + 8$, Fear of Lightning

4. $6n + 3$, Fear of Snakes

5. $4x + 12$, Fear of Fire

6. $4p + 9$, Fear of Heights

7. $6n + 36$, Fear of Water

8. $8x + 28$, Fear of Light

9. $12p + 30$, Fear of Infinity

10. $9n + 12$, Fear of Dirt

Have No Fear

Don't worry—algebra is nothing to fear! But some people do fear specific things, like heights, snakes, or fire. These strong fears are called *phobias*.

To find out what each phobia below means, use the distributive property to simplify each expression. Draw a line to match the expression to its simplest form.

1.	**Zoophobia**	$4n + 2n$	$6n + 36$	**Fear of Water**
2.	**Nyctophobia**	$x + 3x$	$6n + 3$	**Fear of Snakes**
3.	**Astraphobia**	$p + 8 + 7p$	$8x + 28$	**Fear of Light**
4.	**Ophidiophobia**	$8n + 3 - 2n$	$6n$	**Fear of Animals**
5.	**Pyrophobia**	$4(x + 3)$	$9n + 12$	**Fear of Dirt**
6.	**Acrophobia**	$6p + 17 - 8 - 2p$	$12p + 30$	**Fear of Infinity**
7.	**Hydrophobia**	$3(n + 6) + 3(n + 6)$	$4p + 9$	**Fear of Heights**
8.	**Photophobia**	$7(2x + 4) - 6x$	$4x + 12$	**Fear of Fire**
9.	**Apeirophobia**	$5(2p + 6) + 2p$	$4x$	**Fear of Darkness**
10.	**Mysophobia**	$n(6 + 3) + 12$	$8p + 8$	**Fear of Lightning**

Algebra Readiness Scholastic Professional Books

Order Up!

Waiter! We'll have a large order of operations, with a helping of diner slang on the side.

➔ Directions

1. Duplicate a copy of the *Order Up!* reproducible for each student.

2. Review the rules for order of operations with students:

   a. First, do the math that's inside parentheses.

   b. Next, do the multiplication and division.

   c. Finally, do the addition and subtraction.

   Remember: Do each step from left to right. If there is more than one case of multiplication or division, do the problem on the left first, then move to the next problem on the right, and so on.

3. Go over the example on the reproducible with students. Have them redo the problem on paper, but this time do the operations in a different order. How many different answers can they find? Ask a volunteer to demonstrate his or her alternative answers on the board. Encourage students to discuss why order of operations is useful to ensure that everyone gets the same answer for a math problem.

4. Instruct students to complete the page on their own. If you like, they may use calculators to do the computation.

★ Taking It Farther

✳ Have each student pick his or her favorite food from the list and make up a new series of operations that will yield that number. A classmate can do the math to find out which food was picked.

✳ Students may also use current teen expressions to make up their own order of operations puzzle. Or they may research jargon used by other groups such as surfers, snowboarders, or workers in a parent's or a relative's profession.

✔ Assessing Skills

If there is more than one operation contained within parentheses, do students still follow order of operations?

Order Up!

"Hey Louie—give me a British!" a waiter yells to the cook in a restaurant. He's using "diner slang" to say he needs an English muffin. Diner slang is a fast way to describe food orders. Plus, it's funny! To find out what other diner slang means, place your order for order of operations! The example below will show you how.

Diner Slang

52	Poached eggs on an English muffin
79	Corned beef hash
61	Orange juice
4	Crackers
18	Hot dogs
38	Water
208	Chili

EXAMPLE: $27 + 5 - (4 \div 2) \times 7$ "I need three bun pups!"

* First, do the math in parentheses: $27 + 5 - 2 \times 7$
* Then, do the multiplication: $27 + 5 - 14$
* Finally, do the addition and subtraction, from left to right: $32 - 14$
* Answer: 18

Find your answer in the Diner Slang box. The food listed next to the correct number tells you what the order was for: Hot dogs.

Now, take a bite out of these unusual-sounding food orders!

A. $72 \times 3 - 8$ "Give me two bowls of red!"

This order is for 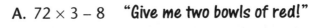.

B. $288 \div 12 \times 3 + 7$ "Clean up the kitchen!"

This order is for 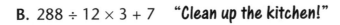.

C. $42 - (2 \times 6) \div 3$ "Pour out three glasses of city juice!"

This order is for _____.

D. $20 \times (7 - 2) - (8 \times 6)$ "Give me an Adam and Eve on a raft!"

This order is for _____.

E. $(12 - 32 \div 8) \div 2$ "Where are those dog biscuits?"

This order is for _____.

F. $(2 + 12 \times 10) \div (11 - 9)$ "I need a squeeze!"

This order is for _____.

Algebra Readiness Scholastic Professional Books

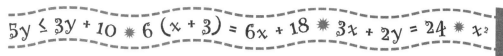

Numbers of Invention

Which came first, calculators or frozen food? This number line will get students plugged in to some of the world's greatest inventions!

Directions

1. Duplicate the *Numbers of Invention* reproducible for each student.

2. Review number lines and positive and negative numbers. Remind students that the greater a number is, the farther to the right it is on the number line.

3. Draw the following number line on the board:

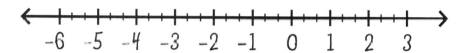

4. Call on volunteers to plot the points $1\frac{2}{3}$, -3, and $-5\frac{1}{3}$ on the number line.

5. Ask students: *Which number is the greatest? Which number is the least? How do you know?*

6. Have students complete the reproducible on their own.

Taking It Farther

Challenge each student to create a number line similar to the one in the activity but based on events in his or her own life. Partners can then trade puzzles and solve them to find the order of events.

Assessing Skills

* Do students understand that −3 is greater than −5?
* Note whether students plot negative fractions correctly, to the left of the negative whole number.

LEARNING OBJECTIVE

Students plot points on a number line.

GROUPING

Individual

MATERIALS

* *Numbers of Invention* reproducible (p. 18)

ANSWERS

Calculator, 1833

Telephone, 1876

Car, 1889

Toaster, 1918

Frozen Food, 1924

Television, 1927

Computer, 1944

Tupperware, 1945

Velcro, 1948

Audiocassette, 1963

Video Game, 1972

Date _____

Numbers of Invention

Over the years, scientists have come up with some terrific ideas. Today, it's pretty hard to imagine life without such wonders as computers, video games, or even Velcro.

Which of these inventions came first? Plot some points on a number line to find out! After you mark each point, write the name of the invention underneath. One is done for you. The inventions will go from earliest to most recent, from left to right along the number line.

Inventions

$-3\frac{3}{4}$ Car	$2\frac{7}{8}$ Velcro
-2 Frozen Food	$-\frac{5}{8}$ Television
$4\frac{1}{2}$ Audiocassette	$-3\frac{1}{8}$ Toaster
$-4\frac{1}{2}$ Telephone	$1\frac{1}{8}$ Tupperware
$5\frac{5}{8}$ Video Game	$-5\frac{3}{8}$ Calculator
$\frac{1}{4}$ Computer	

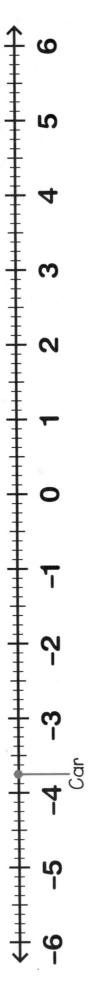

Car

Year each invention appeared, in order on the number line from least to greatest:
1833, 1876, 1889, 1918, 1924, 1927, 1944, 1945, 1948, 1963, 1972

Write the name of each invention and the year it appeared.

_____

_____

_____

_____

Inequality Mix-Up

When half the students in your class search for the student whose graph matches their inequality, the result equals fun!

◉→ Directions

1. Review the symbols $>$, $\geq$, $<$, and $\leq$. Remind students that inequalities using these symbols can be solved much the same as an equation.

2. Write the following inequality on the board:
$$-5x - 4 < 11$$
$$-5x - 4 + 4 < 11 + 4$$
$$-5x < 15$$
$$-5x/-5 < 15/-5$$
$$x > -3$$

   Ask volunteers to go though each step to solve it, or write and explain each step yourself. Note that when you divide by a negative number, you must reverse the inequality symbol.

3. On the board, graph the solution on a number line:

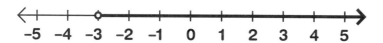

4. If the plotted point is filled in, it represents a number. If the solution to the inequality were $x \geq -3$, the graph would be as follows:

   ← | -5 -4 -3 -2 -1 0 1 2 3 4 5 | →

5. Distribute one index card to each student. Half the cards should have an inequality written on them. The other half should show the graph of the solution.

6. Have each student with an inequality card find the student who has the matching graphed solution.

☆ Taking It Farther

Ask each student to create and graph his or her own inequality on two index cards. You now have enough inequality cards to play the game two more times!

✓ Assessing Skills

Do students understand the difference between graphing $>$ and $\geq$, and the difference between graphing $<$ and $\leq$?

LEARNING OBJECTIVE
Students solve and graph inequalities.

GROUPING
Whole class

MATERIALS
✳ index card for each student

ADVANCE PREPARATION
Write inequalities and their corresponding graphed solutions on different index cards. Each student should receive one card. Here are examples of some inequalities you may want to use:

$$x + 2 \geq 7$$
$$3n < -9$$
$$15y + 8 > 9y + 20$$
$$4b - 7 < 9$$
$$2(c - 3) > -2$$
$$5j \leq 3j + 10$$
$$-3m \geq 6$$
$$-4h - 3 > 17$$
$$t + 3 < 5$$
$$4 + 7r - 6 > 5$$
$$p - 21 \leq -21$$
$$8w + 7 \geq 55$$

Amazing Animal Inequalities

Get ready for some animal facts that are really wild! Students work with inequalities to figure out which statements are true.

⟳→ Directions

1. Duplicate the *Amazing Animal Inequalities* reproducible for each student.

2. Review the inequality symbols >, <, ≥, and ≤ with students. Emphasize that for an inequality statement to be true, the smaller end of the symbol must point to the smaller number.

3. Write the following inequality statements on the board:

$$x + 5 < 8$$
$$2y - 3 \geq 12$$

For each inequality, ask volunteers to find values for *x* and *y* that make the statement true. Then have them identify values for *x* and *y* that make the statement false.

4. Distribute the reproducible and let students complete it on their own. If you like, they may use calculators to do the computation.

★ Taking It Farther

Ask each student to do library research on a favorite animal, making a list of interesting facts about the animal. Then they use their imaginations to come up with false statements about the animals. To accompany their statements, they can write true and false inequalities for classmates to solve.

✔ Assessing Skills

Note whether students reverse the greater than and less than signs when evaluating the inequalities.

LEARNING OBJECTIVE

Students evaluate inequalities.

GROUPING

Individual

MATERIALS

✳ *Amazing Animal Inequalities* reproducible (p. 21)

✳ calculators (optional)

ANSWERS

1. True
2. True
3. True
4. True
5. False
6. False
7. True
8. True
9. True
10. False

Amazing Animal Inequalities

Below you'll find some incredible facts about animals. But only some of them are true!
To find out which statements are just hogwash, look at each inequality. If the inequality
is true, so is the fact. Circle True. If the inequality is false, the statement is too. Circle False.

1. Some types of bats measure just one inch long.

   True or False?

   $2x - 14 \leq 8,\ x = 11$

2. There are at least 1,000,000 insects for every human being on Earth!

   True or False?

   $16 < 3t + 8,\ t = 3$

3. Ostriches spend 10 hours per day hiding their heads in holes in the ground.

   True or False?

   $12 < 5r + 4,\ r = 2$

4. In England, "Beano" is one of the top ten names for pet dogs.

   True or False?

   $4c + c - 6 \geq 15,\ c = 5$

5. A giant South American species of rabbit can weigh up to 275 pounds.

   True or False?

   $o + 14 - 2o \leq 12,\ o = 1$

6. One of the top ten names for pet goldfish in the U.S. is "Fluffy."

   True or False?

   $u \div 12 \geq 3,\ u = 24$

7. Blue whales weigh as much as 260,000 pounds.

   True or False?

   $20 > 7 + 4j,\ j = 2$

8. Some clams live up to 200 years.

   True or False?

   $15 \geq 18 - 3z,\ z = 1$

9. Koalas are the laziest animals in the world. They snooze 22 hours per day.

   True or False?

   $4y + 6 + 3y < 50,\ y = 6$

10. The amazing cheetah can run 120 miles per hour.

    True or False?

    $3p - 12 > 0,\ p = 4$

Happy Birth Day!

On which day of the week were you born? Using this handy formula, students will find out in less time than it takes to sing "Happy Birthday to Me!"

➜ Directions

1. Explain to students that they will use a formula to find out on which day of the week they were born. Write this formula on the board:

$$\text{Birth Day } (b) = \frac{y + d + f}{7}$$

Let y equal the year that you were born.

Let d equal the day of the year you were born, from 1 to 366.

Let f equal $\frac{y - 1}{4}$.   Ignore the remainder and just use the whole number for f.

2. You may want to go over the following example first and work through each step as a class.

   Juana was born on April 15, 1984, which is a leap year. (Remember that February has 29 days in a leap year. Any year that is evenly divisible by 4 is a leap year.)

   a. Add 31 (days in January) + 29 (days in February) + 31 (days in March) + 15 (days in April) = 106.

   b. Plug in the values for y, d, and f into the formula for b. Do the division without a calculator to find the remainder.

   $$\frac{1984 + 106 + 495}{7} = 369 \text{ R2}$$

   c. Use the remainder to find out on which day you were born. Write the following on the board as a reference:

   0 = Friday   1 = Saturday   2 = Sunday   3 = Monday
   4 = Tuesday   5 = Wednesday   6 = Thursday

   d. Since Juana's remainder is 2, April 15, 1984, was a Sunday.

3. Have each student use his or her birthday to work through the steps.

☆ Taking It Farther

Have students find the birth day for members of their families. Also, encourage them to research the birthdays of their favorite sports and media celebrities and use the formula to find their birth days.

✓ Assessing Skills

Ask students to explain the formula in their own words. Are they able to describe what each variable stands for?

LEARNING OBJECTIVE
Students use a formula.

GROUPING
Individual

MATERIALS
✳ paper and pencil
✳ calculator

The Shadow Knows

How tall is your school building? Students don't have to climb it to find out. Just wait for a sunny day, head outside, and use this formula!

Directions

1. Make sure it is a sunny day. Explain to students that they will be using shadows to find the heights of tall objects. Have them write the following formula at the top of their papers:

$$\frac{\text{Stick Length} \times \text{Object Shadow}}{\text{Stick Shadow}} = \text{Object Height}$$

2. Take the class outside. Instruct students to hold the yardstick or meter stick straight up, touching the ground. Using the measuring tape or the other yardstick, have them measure the shadow cast along the ground by the upright yardstick.

3. Next, ask students to use the measuring tape or yardstick to measure the shadows cast by several tall objects, such as your school building, a flagpole, or a tree.

4. Students should use their measurements and the formula to find the heights of the objects. You may want to let them use calculators to do the computation.

Taking It Farther

✻ Have students check that the formula works by measuring their own shadows and using the formula to find their own heights.

✻ Ask students: *Why would you get an inaccurate answer if you measured the yardstick's shadow at 9:00 A.M. and then measured a tree's shadow at 11:30 A.M.?* [Because the sun would be higher in the sky at 11:30 A.M., shortening the length of the tree's shadow. This formula is based on the following ratio: $\frac{\text{Stick Length}}{\text{Stick Shadow}} = \frac{\text{Object Height}}{\text{Object Shadow}}$.]

Assessing Skills

Do students convert all measurements into the same units (such as inches or centimeters) before they plug the numbers into the formula?

LEARNING OBJECTIVE
Students practice using a formula.

GROUPING
Whole class

MATERIALS
✻ paper and pencil
✻ yardstick or meterstick
✻ measuring tape (or another yardstick)
✻ calculators (optional)

Bone Up on Formulas

Make no bones about it—students will get a thrill out of finding out how forensic scientists use formulas to do their jobs!

⟶ Directions

1. Duplicate the *Bone Up on Formulas* reproducible for each student.

2. If necessary, review the terms *variable* and *formula* with the class.

3. Explain to students that they will be using formulas that are part of a forensic scientist's job. Scientists use these formulas to find out more about old bones or bones related to crimes.

4. Let students complete the activity on their own. If they are not yet comfortable using formulas, you may want to go over the first one or two questions with the entire class first.

☆ Taking It Farther

✳ Remind students that all measurements in the activity are in centimeters. To get an idea of how tall each person mentioned in the activity really is, have them convert measurements into meters or feet and inches.

✳ Challenge students to find other jobs in which formulas are used. They may interview family members or do research in a library. Examples include retail sales (in which sale prices and stock needs may be calculated with a formula), accounting (tax rates), and truck driving (using the formula for rate to estimate how long it will take to drive a given distance). Then ask each student to interview an adult who uses formulas on the job. Students can present their findings in class, and even invite the adult to visit the class and answer questions about his or her job.

✓ Assessing Skills

Note whether students understand the difference among the variables r, h, and t, and employ the correct formula for each question.

LEARNING OBJECTIVE
Students practice using a formula.

GROUPING
Whole class

MATERIALS
✳ *Bone Up on Formulas* reproducible (p. 25)
✳ calculators (optional)

ANSWERS
1. $72.6 + 2.5t$ = height
2. 165.1 cm
3. 192.1 cm
4. 151.8 cm
5. 195.1 cm

Bone Up on Formulas

To a forensic scientist, a skeleton isn't just a pile of old bones. It's a clue! Sometimes, a scientist may have only one bone to study. But thanks to formulas, even that can be enough to find out information such as how tall the person was when he or she was alive.

Take a look at the real-life forensic formulas below. Then use them to answer the questions.

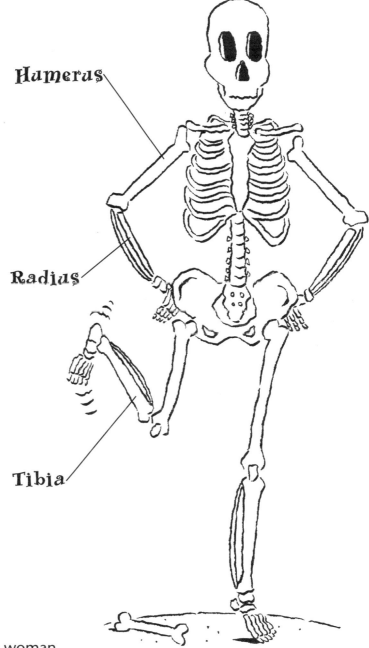

Hamerus

Radius

Tibia

Forensic Formulas for Height

In these formulas, r = radius, h = humerus, and t = tibia. All measurements are in centimeters (cm).

MALE:	$80.4 + 3.7r$ = height
	$73.6 + 3.0h$ = height
	$81.7 + 2.4t$ = height
FEMALE:	$73.5 + 3.9r$ = height
	$65.0 + 3.1h$ = height
	$72.6 + 2.5t$ = height

1. A forensic scientist is given the tibia of a woman who lived hundreds of years ago, found at an archaeological dig. What formula should the scientist use to find out how tall the woman was? _____

2. If the tibia from question 1 was 37 cm long, how tall was the woman? _____

3. Suppose police find a man's tibia that is 46 cm long. How tall was he? _____

4. Say a woman's humerus, 28 cm long, is discovered. How tall was she? _____

5. A forensic scientist finds a man's radius, 31 cm long. How tall was he? _____

Party on with Variables!

Real-life math meets real-life fun as students use prealgebra skills to plan a party.

⟳→ Directions

1. Start by reviewing the term *variables* and tell students they'll be using variables to plan a fictional party. Discuss the many variables involved in party planning, including number of guests to invite, types of food and beverages, and decorations.

2. Have students suggest items to buy for the party. Write the list of items on the board, and assign a letter variable to each item. For example, *p* could be used to represent pizzas, and *c* to represent bags of chips.

3. Discuss the number of guests to invite. Once the class has decided, begin writing expressions on the board showing how many of each item will be needed. Say there will be 30 guests, and you want to have one bag of chips for every 3 guests. The expression for the number of bags of chips needed is $10c$. Ask volunteers to write expressions for the remaining items on the board.

4. Next, write an estimated cost for an item on the board, such as $c = \$1.69$. Explain that this means one bag of chips costs $1.69.

5. Have pairs estimate costs for the remaining items. Using these estimates, students evaluate the expressions. What will be the total cost of the party? Ask students to compare and discuss their answers.

☆ Taking It Farther

Let students research the actual prices of items for their party, finding prices for different brands of the same item, different types of foods, and so on. They may work in groups, where each group member is responsible for researching a different item. Then each group evaluates the expressions using the real-life prices and compares the total party costs if different brands are purchased. If possible, you may even have students use this method to plan a real holiday or end-of-the-year party.

✔ Assessing Skills

✳ Observe whether students can explain the reasoning behind the expressions they write. Do they understand that $10c$ means $10 \times c$?

✳ Two items may begin with the same letter. Do students realize that they must then assign a different variable to the second item?

LEARNING OBJECTIVE
Students use variables to write and evaluate expressions.

GROUPING
Whole class, pairs

MATERIALS
✳ paper and pencil

Variable Bingo

Students will invariably have a great time as they play this game. Plus they'll get lots of practice using variables.

➤ Directions

1. Duplicate the *Variable Bingo* reproducible. Distribute one copy to each student.

2. Ask students to randomly fill in each square on their bingo cards with one of the bingo numbers.

3. Draw a slip of paper out of the paper bag, calling out the letter and number that you drew. The letter tells students which expression to evaluate. The number tells them what value to substitute for the variable in that expression. For example, if you call B4, students should substitute the number 4 for *n* in Expression B: $n + 21$. The solution is 25.

4. Students look for that solution on their bingo cards. If the number is there, they draw an X over it.

5. Continue drawing slips of paper and have students solve the equations. The first student to get four across, down, or diagonally wins.

6. Play the game again, with students choosing different numbers for their bingo cards.

✪ Taking It Farther

As a more difficult way to play the game, have students randomly write A1, A2, A3, A4, A5, A6, B1, B2, and so on in their bingo squares. Then write the solution numbers (the bingo numbers listed on the reproducible) on 24 slips of paper, and draw those from the bag. When you call out a number, students must figure out which variable value was used with which expression to get that number.

✔ Assessing Skills

✱ Do students use estimation to check the reasonableness of their solutions?

✱ If the solution is not on their cards, note whether students check the bingo number list to make sure it is one of the possible solutions.

LEARNING OBJECTIVE

Students substitute different values for variables.

GROUPING

Whole class

MATERIALS

✱ *Variable Bingo* reproducible (p. 28) (2 copies for each student)

✱ 24 slips of paper

✱ paper bag or other container

ADVANCE PREPARATION

On each of the 24 slips of paper, write one of the following: A1, A2, A3, A4, A5, A6, B1, B2, B3, B4, B5, B6, C1, C2, C3, C4, C5, C6, D1, D2, D3, D4, D5, D6.

Put the slips of paper in the paper bag.

Variable Bingo

Write one of the bingo numbers in each square.
Use a different number in each square.

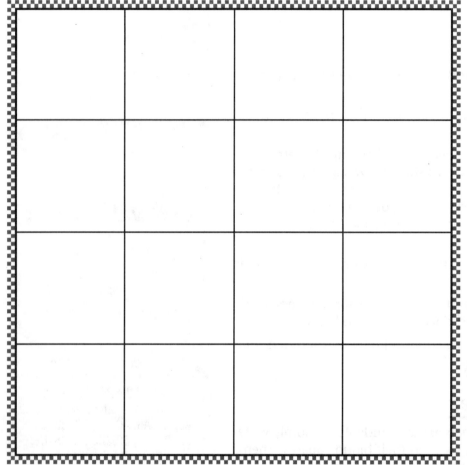

Bingo Numbers

0	3	4	6	7	9
10	12	13	15	16	19
22	23	24	25	26	27
29	31	33	35	37	39

EXPRESSION A: $3x - 3$

EXPRESSION B: $n + 21$

EXPRESSION C: $22 - 3k$

EXPRESSION D: $27 + 2p$

WORK SPACE

Magical Memorizing Math Teacher

Use this memory trick on students, and they'll be in for a treat when they use variables and the distributive property to see how it works!

➤ Directions

1. When class begins, tell students that you have memorized an entire textbook. Tell them you will prove it, but that they will have to do some math first.

2. Ask students for a three-digit number. Write the number on the board. Reverse the three digits, and subtract the smaller number from the larger number.

3. The difference will be one of the following numbers: 0, 99, 198, 297, 396, 495, 594, 693, 792, or 891. If the number is within the range of your textbook's pages, tell students to turn to that page while you magically tell them, without looking, the last word on that page. If the answer is 0 or a number that is too high, try again.

4. Repeat the test until it becomes evident that the same numbers are coming up again and again. Then do the following proof to show how the trick works.

5. Tell the class you will use variable letters to represent the digits in the problem. Use x for the hundreds place, y for the tens place, and z for the ones place. Therefore, the first 3-digit number can be written: $100x + 10y + z$. (If students are confused, give them a concrete example, such as $327 = 300 + 20 + 7$.)

6. When the digits are reversed, you get $100z + 10y + x$. What happens now? Assume x is greater than z. When you take $100x + 10y + z$ and subtract $100z + 10y + x$, the answer is $99x - 99z$. With the distributive property, that becomes $99(x - z)$.

7. Since x and z are single-digit numbers, the difference between them will be 0, 1, 2, 3, 4, 5, 6, 7, 8, or 9. (This will be the same whether x or z is greater.) When you multiply these digits by 99, you will get the ten numbers listed above.

☆ Taking It Farther

Have students research other algebra proofs and present an explanation of them to the class.

✔ Assessing Skills

Challenge students to write step-by-step descriptions, in their own words, of how the above proof works.

LEARNING OBJECTIVE

Students use variables and the distributive property to understand an algebra proof.

GROUPING

Whole class

MATERIALS

✹ math textbook (or any other textbook)

ADVANCE PREPARATION

Before class, memorize the last word on the following pages of the textbook: 99, 198, 297, 396, 495, 594. (If your book is very long, also memorize the last word on the following pages: 693, 792, 891.) If you don't want to memorize the words, write out a small "cheat sheet" that can be hidden in your hand.

Train Trouble

Every stop on this train will give students more fun practice with variables!

⟳→ Directions

1. Duplicate the *Train Trouble* reproducible for each group.

2. Divide the class into groups of 3 or 4. Instruct groups to cut out the spinners on the reproducible.

3. Players place their markers on Start and spin to see who goes first. To use the spinner, they spin the paper clip around the point of a pencil.

4. For their first turn, players spin to see how many spaces to move. On each succeeding turn, players spin and then evaluate the expression on the space by substituting the number spun for the variable. If the answer is a positive number, the player moves that many spaces forward. If it is a negative number, the player moves that many spaces backward.

5. Here is an example you may use to explain game play to students. *Say your marker is on the space* r – 3. *If you spin a 1, your answer will be –2, and you must move back 2 spaces. If you spin a 4, your answer will be 1, so you move forward 1 space.*

6. The first player to pass the Finish space wins. It is not necessary to reach Finish on an exact number.

☆ Taking It Farther

After playing the game a few times, ask students to predict what would happen if the spinner were changed to show the numbers 1–8. Students can trace the spinner on the reproducible and divide it into 8 equal sections. After labeling the sections from 1 to 8, they can cut out the spinner and use it to play the game again to test their theories.

✔ Assessing Skills

Observe whether students have difficulty evaluating the expressions when the answer is a negative number.

LEARNING OBJECTIVE

Students substitute numeric values for variables.

GROUPING

Cooperative groups of 3 or 4

MATERIALS

✳ *Train Trouble* reproducible (p. 31)

✳ different-colored game markers for each student

✳ scrap paper

✳ scissors, pencil, and paper clip (to make the spinner)

Train Trouble

All aboard! The *Algebra Express* train is about to depart. Unfortunately, the train is overdue for repairs. Sometimes it travels fast, sometimes it travels slowly, and sometimes it even travels backward! Better get that train to the repair shop . . . and step on it!

VARIABLE SPINNER

Start

$3n - 3$

$2c - 2$

$-1 + 2x$

$7 - 2j$

$v + 2$

$r - 3$

$10 - q^2$

$9 - 4m$

$3t - 7$

$-8 + s$

$9 - p$

$2k - 5$

$-4 + 2y$

$-2 + w$

$z^2 - 5$

Trent 'n' Trina's Train Repair Shop

Finish

Express Yourself

How do students' favorite stars of sports, music, and movies express themselves? Evaluate expressions to find out!

➜ Directions

1. Duplicate the *Express Yourself* reproducible for each student.

2. Review the term *expression* with students and remind them that expressions are evaluated. The evaluation of an expression will change if you change the value of any of the variables in the expression. On the board, write the following expression from question 1 of the *Express Yourself* reproducible: $6m + 3$.

3. Go over the example using the value $m = 7$ from the reproducible. Ask a volunteer to evaluate the expression again, using a different value for m.

4. Let students complete the page on their own. You may want to have them use calculators to do the computation for each problem.

☆ Taking It Farther

What happens when you substitute different values for the variables in the activity? Encourage students to pick one of the single-variable expressions on the reproducible and evaluate it where the variable = 1, 2, 3, and so on. (Students should round their answers to the nearest hundredth.) What pattern is evident? Students can compare their answers, explaining how they think different operations such as division and multiplication affected their results.

✔ Assessing Skills

✳ In cases where there is more than one variable, note whether students substitute the correct value for the correct variable.

✳ Are students applying knowledge of order of operations to evaluate the expressions correctly?

LEARNING OBJECTIVE

Students evaluate expressions when given values for variables.

GROUPING

Individual

MATERIALS

✳ *Express Yourself* reproducible (p. 33)

✳ calculators (optional)

ANSWERS

2. 20, "I feel a little ridiculous."

3. 10.68, "I always liked math."

4. 37.8, "I have a nervous stomach."

5. 20.55, "I used to eat mayonnaise sandwiches."

6. 54, "I'm not a couch potato."

7. 30, "I think it's OK to be a movie star."

8. 24.18, "I'm such a mall rat."

Express Yourself

You probably have a lot on your mind. Well, so do the famous people listed on this page! Each of them made one of the statements in the box. Who said what?

To find out, evaluate the expression above each celebrity's name. Then find your answer next to a quote in the Answer Box. Write the quote in the blank. We did the first one for you.

Answer Box

10.68   "I always liked math."
54   "I'm not a couch potato."
20.55   "I used to eat mayonnaise sandwiches."
45   "I always wanted to go in the space shuttle."
24.18   "I'm such a mall rat."
30   "I think it's OK to be a movie star."
37.8   "I have a nervous stomach."
20   "I feel a little ridiculous."

1. Evaluate $6m + 3$, where $m = 7$.

   Substitute 7 for m: $6 \times 7 + 3 = 45$.

   Actor Will Smith said: _"I always wanted to go in the space shuttle."_

2. Evaluate $4p$, where $p = 5$.

   Actress Claire Danes said: _____

3. Evaluate $7i - 12$, where $i = 3.24$.

   Basketball star Scottie Pippen said: _____

4. Evaluate $r + 3t$, where $r = 0.9$ and $t = 12.3$.

   Actor Brad Pitt said: _____

5. Evaluate $25.75k - 12m$, where $k = 9$ and $m = 17.6$.

   Actress Jennifer Aniston said: _____

6. Evaluate $23 + 4.8z - y$, where $z = 7.5$ and $y = 5$.

   Football star Jerry Rice said: _____

7. Evaluate $6j \div 3.07$, where $j = 15.35$.

   Actress Winona Ryder said: _____

8. Evaluate $4.004 + 8g \div 0.5e$, where $g = 12.61$ and $e = 10$.

   Singer Darius Rucker of Hootie and the Blowfish said: _____

Equations Are the Name of the Game!

Do students love basketball? Here's an equation that can help sports fans really know the score!

⟩ Directions

1. Ask a student who is familiar with basketball to explain the sport's 2- and 3-point shot scoring system.

2. Many box scores list a player's total number of field goals scored (with both 2- and 3-point shots included), number of 3-point shots scored, and total points scored. They do not list 2-point shots scored. (Box score formats may vary. If your newspaper does itemize 2-point shots, leave out that number when you give the information for this activity to students.)

3. Ask students: *Using the numbers from the box score, how could you find out how many 2-point field goals a player scored in a game?* After some discussion, they should find that they can multiply the number of 3-point shots scored by 3, subtract the product from the total number of points scored, and divide the difference by 2.

4. Challenge students to make this process easier by writing an equation to describe the number of 2-point shots, 3-point shots, and total points scored. They should start by assigning a variable to describe 2-point shots and another variable to describe 3-point shots. After some discussion, they should come up with this equation or a variation of it:

    If t = total points, p = 2-point shots, and q = 3-point shots, then: $t = 2p + 3q$.

5. Allow time for students to plug numbers from several box scores into their equations.

★ Taking It Farther

What other equations can be used in determining sports scores? Hold a class discussion, asking students who are sports fans to share their knowledge to help identify equations.

✓ Assessing Skills

In the equation, do students understand why one variable is multiplied by 2, while one is multiplied by 3? Ask them to explain in their own words.

LEARNING OBJECTIVE

Students use equations to solve an everyday problem.

GROUPING

Whole class

MATERIALS

✳ sports section of a newspaper, showing box scores from basketball games (Note: This activity should be done during basketball season.)

The Amazin' Equation Game

Get ready for do-it-yourself math, as students make up equations for classmates to solve.

⟳→ Directions

1. Duplicate the *The Amazin' Equation Game* reproducible for each student.

2. If necessary, review how to use inverse operations to solve simple equations of the form $x + a = b$ or $b = x + a$.

3. Divide the class into groups. One student will be the master of ceremonies (MC), while the other students are the players.

4. Direct students to cut out the spinners on the reproducible. To begin a round, the MC spins the number spinner four times and then spins the operations spinner two times. Each player writes the four digits and two operations (− or +) spun in the spaces for Round 1.

5. Each player now creates an equation using the four digits and the two operations. The equation should be of the form $x + a = b$ or $b = x + a$. For example, the following digits and operations are spun: 7, 3, 0, 8, −, +. Three possible equations that could be made are:

   $$80 = x + (-37) \qquad x - 8 = 70 + 3 \qquad -308 = x + 7$$

6. Now, each player passes his or her reproducible to the player on the left. Players solve the equations they are given, with the player who wrote each equation checking the answer. Each player who solves an equation correctly gets one point. The MC keeps score.

7. For rounds 2 through 4, students alternate passing their equations to the right and to the left. Whoever has the most points after four rounds is the winner.

☆ Taking It Farther

To make the game harder, white-out one + and one − on the operations spinner on a duplicate of the reproducible. Write × and ÷ in their place and duplicate the revised reproducible. Note: In this version of the game, some equations may yield long decimal answers. You may want to have students use calculators and round answers to the nearest hundredth or thousandth.

✓ Assessing Skills

Note whether students are able to think of several different types of equations. Also, observe whether they have difficulty solving equations in which the variable is to the right of the equal sign.

LEARNING OBJECTIVE

Students write and solve equations.

GROUPING

Cooperative groups of 3 to 5

MATERIALS

✳ *The Amazin' Equation Game* reproducible (p. 36)

✳ scrap paper and pencil

✳ scissors and a paper clip for each group (to make the spinner)

✳ calculators (optional)

The Amazin' Equation Game

ROUND 1

Numbers: ☐ ☐ ☐ ☐

Operations: ☐ ☐

Equation: _____

Solution: *x* = _____

ROUND 2

Numbers: ☐ ☐ ☐ ☐

Operations: ☐ ☐

Equation: _____

Solution: *x* = _____

ROUND 3

Numbers: ☐ ☐ ☐ ☐

Operations: ☐ ☐

Equation: _____

Solution: *x* = _____

ROUND 4

Numbers: ☐ ☐ ☐ ☐

Operations: ☐ ☐

Equation: _____

Solution: *x* = _____

NUMBERS SPINNER

OPERATIONS SPINNER

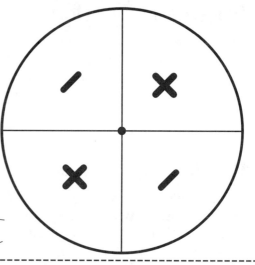

Algebra Readiness Scholastic Professional Books

On Sale Now—Algebra!

In this real-life math activity, students use equations to discover how much they'd pay in finance charges if they bought a product on an installment plan.

⟿ Directions

1. A few weeks before doing the activity, ask students to look for ads for products that offer the option of full payment or payment by an installment plan. They may also write this information for products shown in television ads or infomercials. If students have an older sibling who has taken out a loan to pay for college, they can also use information from the student loan repayment plan.

2. Once you have collected a few advertisements, you're ready to do the activity.

3. Go over the term *finance charge*. Can students explain what a finance charge is?

4. Write the following equation on the board:

   Cash price (*c*) = Installment plan price (*i*) − Finance charge (*f*)

5. Write the information from an ad on the board. Ask a volunteer to come up and use the information to plug the cash price and the installment plan price into the equation. (The student will have to multiply the amount of one installment payment by the number of payments required.)

6. Next, call on another volunteer to solve the equation and determine the finance charge.

7. Repeat the activity for all the advertisements collected.

☆ Taking It Farther

Ask students: *Would you ever consider buying something on an installment plan? Why or why not? What are some pros and cons to buying on an installment plan?* Have students write a paragraph that refers to the results of the class activity.

✓ Assessing Skills

Observe to see if students use estimation to check whether their answers make sense.

LEARNING OBJECTIVE

Students solve equations and see how prealgebra can be used in everyday life.

GROUPING

Whole class

MATERIALS

✳ newspaper and magazine ads, store circulars, and so on, showing installment plan prices and cash prices for products such as stereo systems, cars, and kitchen appliances

Step "Two" It!

Students solve two-step equations to find out who stole Two-Step Tony's tap shoes!

Directions

1. Duplicate the *Step "Two" It!* reproducible for each student.

2. Review the process of solving two-step equations in class. Here is an example you can write on the board:

$$x + y = 14$$
$$3x - 2y = 2$$

3. Call on a volunteer to solve the equations for x and y, assuming that x and y have the same value in both equations. [$x = 6$, $y = 8$]

4. If students have trouble with the example, go through the steps on the board of one possible solution:

   a. Use inverse operations to rewrite the first equation:
   $$x = 14 - y$$

   b. Substitute for x in the second equation:
   $$3(14 - y) - 2y = 2$$

   c. Solve for y:
   $$42 - 3y - 2y = 2$$
   $$40 = 5y$$
   $$8 = y$$

   d. Use the value for y to solve for x:
   $$x + 8 = 14, \text{ so } x = 6$$

   e. Check that your answer is correct by plugging the values for x and y into both equations to see if they work.

5. Distribute the reproducible and let students complete it on their own. They should have plenty of scrap paper for doing the calculations. If you like, they may also use calculators to do the computation.

☆ Taking It Farther

Challenge students to write their own two-step equations for classmates to solve.

✔ Assessing Skills

Observe whether students make correct use of the distributive property when substituting values for a variable. For example, in the problem above, $3(14 - y)$ becomes $42 - 3y$. Also, what do students do if the values they find for x and y do not work in the original equations?

LEARNING OBJECTIVE

Students solve two-step equations.

GROUPING

Individual

MATERIALS

* *Step "Two" It!* reproducible (p. 39)
* scrap paper and pencil
* calculators (optional)

ANSWERS

A. $x = 10$, $y = 7$

B. $x = 5$, $y = 11$

C. $x = 22$, $y = 36$
   Al Steelz is the thief.

Step "Two" It!

Trouble in Tinsel Town! Someone has stolen the famous dancer Two-Step Tony's tap shoes! To taunt poor Tony, the thief left a clue—some two-step equations.

First, solve the two-step equations to find the values of x and y. Then, look for those numbers on the lineup of suspects below.

A. $x - y = 3$ ANSWER: $x = $ _____

$4y + x = 38$ $y = $ _____

B. $2x + 4y = 54$ ANSWER: $x = $ _____

$23 = 3y - 2x$ $y = $ _____

C. $y - 3x = -30$ ANSWER: $x = $ _____

$x + 2y = 94$ $y = $ _____

Circle the suspect who is carrying or wearing all six numbers. That person is the thief!

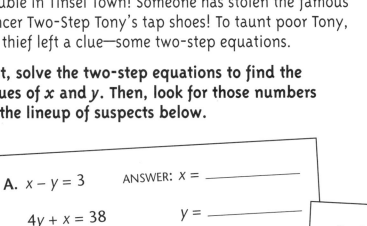

Suspect: Al Steelz   Suspect: Kat Bergler   Suspect: Hy Diditt

Factor Falls

Factors make a big splash as students try to find their way through a white-water rafting maze.

➜ Directions

1. Duplicate the *Factor Falls* reproducible for each student.

2. Review the term *factor* with students.

3. Write the following list of numbers on the board: 5, 9, 3, 81, 25, 27, 150, 675. Call on volunteers to identify numbers on the list that are factors of other numbers on the list. Then ask them to write more factors of the listed numbers on the board.

4. Have students complete the reproducible on their own.

☆ Taking It Farther

Challenge students to find as many factors as possible for the numbers in the maze. Who can come up with the most factors?

✔ Assessing Skills

Observe whether students use basic multiplication facts and divisibility tests to help them find the correct answers. For example, the number 432 does not end in a 0 or 5, so it is not divisible by 5. When students are trying to find a factor of 432, the number 15 can be automatically ruled out, since any multiple of 15 will also be divisible by 5. Therefore, the other choice listed (12) must be the correct answer.

LEARNING OBJECTIVE

Students identify factors of numbers.

GROUPING

Individual

MATERIALS

✳ *Factor Falls* reproducible (p. 41)

✳ markers or pencils

✳ calculators (optional)

ANSWERS

75 (via 5) 531 (via 9) 345 (via 23) 432 (via 12) 810 (via 135) 986 (via 29) 1,482 (via 57) 2,108 (via 62) Finish

Factor Falls

Are you ready to brave the rapids of Factor Falls?
It's a dangerous ride—and you'll need a strong
knowledge of factors to make it down safely!

At each fork in the path, you'll come to
a rock with a number. To avoid crashing
into the rock, follow the path going
down the falls that contains a factor
of that number. If there is no
path with a factor, you've
made a wrong turn.
Go back and try again.
Trace your path with
a marker or pencil.

Let's Make a Factor!

Who knew factors could be so much fun? As they play this game, students may not even notice that they're practicing factoring and problem solving!

➤ Directions

1. Duplicate the *Let's Make a Factor!* reproducible for each pair.

2. Review the term *factor* with students. You may also want to review common divisibility tests that can be used to easily find factors of numbers (for example, a number is divisible by 5 if it ends in 5 or 0).

3. Divide students into pairs. Direct them to use the spinner as shown on the reproducible. Pairs spin to decide who goes first.

4. Player 2 spins four numbers. Player 1 writes the numbers in the "Numbers Spun" spaces on the score sheet. Then, Player 1 uses three of those numbers in any order to make a 3-digit number. Player 1 writes his or her number in the "My 3-Digit Number" spaces on the score sheet. In the space below, Player 1 writes as many factors as he or she can find for the number. The object is to create a number that has as many factors as possible. If you like, students can use calculators to help them find and check factors. (If there is not enough space on the score sheet, scrap paper can be used to write out the factors.)

5. Now, Player 1 spins four numbers, and Player 2 makes a 3-digit number from them. Player 2 finds as many factors as possible for his or her number.

6. The player who has found more factors after three rounds wins.

★ Taking It Farther

✳ Have students play the game, spinning only three numbers and making a 3-digit number. How does this change the game?

✳ After they play several times, encourage students to write journal entries explaining the strategies they used.

✓ Assessing Skills

Observe whether students are able to find more complex factors of numbers, such as 2-digit factors.

LEARNING OBJECTIVE

Students find factors for 3-digit numbers.

GROUPING

Pairs

MATERIALS

✳ *Let's Make a Factor!* reproducible (p. 43)

✳ pencil and a paper clip for each pair of students (to make the spinner)

✳ calculators (optional)

✳ scrap paper (optional)

Let's Make a Factor!

How many factors can you find?
Start spinning, and find out!

ROUND 1

PLAYER 1

Numbers Spun: ☐ ☐ ☐ ☐

My 3-Digit Number: ☐ ☐ ☐

Factors:

Total Factors Found: _____

PLAYER 2

Numbers Spun: ☐ ☐ ☐ ☐

My 3-Digit Number: ☐ ☐ ☐

Factors:

Total Factors Found: _____

ROUND 2

PLAYER 1

Numbers Spun: ☐ ☐ ☐ ☐

My 3-Digit Number: ☐ ☐ ☐

Factors:

Total Factors Found: _____

PLAYER 2

Numbers Spun: ☐ ☐ ☐ ☐

My 3-Digit Number: ☐ ☐ ☐

Factors:

Total Factors Found: _____

ROUND 3

PLAYER 1

Numbers Spun: ☐ ☐ ☐ ☐

My 3-Digit Number: ☐ ☐ ☐

Factors:

Total Factors Found: _____

PLAYER 2

Numbers Spun: ☐ ☐ ☐ ☐

My 3-Digit Number: ☐ ☐ ☐

Factors:

Total Factors Found: _____

Cool Off with Coordinates

To keep tea from cooling off too fast, should you add milk right away or when you are ready to drink it? This hands-on activity reveals the answer!

⟶ Directions

1. Explain to students that they will be measuring the temperature of tea to find out if it cools off faster when milk is added at once, or if it stays hotter longer when the milk is added after 5 minutes.

2. On graph paper, have students draw x- and y-axes. On the x-axis, they should mark intervals of 30 seconds up to 10 minutes and label the x-axis "Time Elapsed." The y-axis should be marked off in intervals of 10 degrees Fahrenheit to 200 degrees Fahrenheit and labeled "Temperature."

3. Since students will be doing the experiment with two cups of tea, they should draw an identical x- and y-axis for the second experiment.

4. If you have two sugar thermometers and stopwatches, you may divide the class into two groups to do the experiment. The first group pours the tea and notes its temperature every 30 seconds, marking the coordinates on the graph. (One student may be in charge of working the stopwatch, while another measures the temperature, and still others write the coordinates and make the graph.) After 30 seconds, the group pours milk into the cup and keeps measuring the temperature for another 5 minutes. The second group pours the same amount of milk into the cup at the beginning and marks the tea's temperature every 30 seconds for 10 minutes. Afterward, the two groups compare their graphs to see which cup of tea was hotter after 10 minutes.

5. If you only have one stopwatch or thermometer, do the experiment as a class, adding milk after 5 minutes. Then repeat the experiment adding milk right at the beginning.

6. Students should discover that the beverage stays hotter if milk is added at once.

☆ Taking It Farther

Have students repeat the experiment several times. How do results vary? Encourage students to write journal entries explaining the experiment and the results.

✓ Assessing Skills

Do students understand that the first number in an ordered pair relates to the x-axis, while the second number relates to the y-axis? Look for students who mix up the numbers.

LEARNING OBJECTIVE

Students make graphs by plotting coordinates.

GROUPING

Cooperative groups or whole class

MATERIALS

✳ 2 sheets of graph paper
✳ straightedge
✳ 1 or 2 sugar thermometers
✳ 1 or 2 stopwatches
✳ 2 cups of hot tea
✳ milk

Grid Giggles

When students use ordered pairs to decipher the answer to a joke, they'll be laughing all the way to their next math test!

⟳ Directions

1. Duplicate the *Grid Giggles* reproducible for each student.

2. Review ordered pairs. If students need practice before they try the activity, draw a grid on the board and call on volunteers to mark points on the grid based on ordered pairs that you call out.

3. To complete the puzzle on the reproducible, students use the ordered pairs under each blank to find a letter positioned at those coordinates on the grid. When the correct letters are written in each blank, the answer to a math riddle is spelled out.

4. Let students complete the reproducible on their own.

✪ Taking It Farther

Encourage students to write their own math jokes or riddles. Then give them graph paper and ask them to use the joke to create a puzzle like *Grid Giggles* for classmates to solve.

✓ Assessing Skills

Observe whether students are confused by negative numbers in the ordered pairs.

LEARNING OBJECTIVE
Students use ordered pairs to locate points on a grid.

GROUPING
Individual

MATERIALS
* *Grid Giggles* reproducible (p. 46)
* graph paper

ANSWER
BECAUSE HE HAD ORDERED PAIRS! (PEARS)

45

Grid Giggles

Under each blank is an ordered pair. Use the ordered pair to find the correct point on the grid. Write the letter from that point in the blank. When you're done, you will have spelled out the answer to this riddle:

Why did the algebra teacher send back the box of peaches he got in the mail?

ANSWER:

___ ___ ___ ___ ___ ___ ___   ___ ___
(2, –3) (3, 3) (–5, –2) (1, 1) (–1, 1) (–2, 3) (3, 3)   (4, 1) (3, 3)

___ ___ ___   ___ ___ ___ ___ ___ ___ ___
(4, 1) (1, 1) (3, –5)   (5, –3) (–3, –3) (3, –5) (3, 3) (–3, –3) (3, 3) (3, –5)

___ ___ ___ ___ ___! (___ ___ ___ ___ ___)
(–3, –5) (1, 1) (–4, 1) (–3, –3) (–2, 3)   (–3, –5) (3, 3) (1, 1) (–3, –3) (–2, 3)

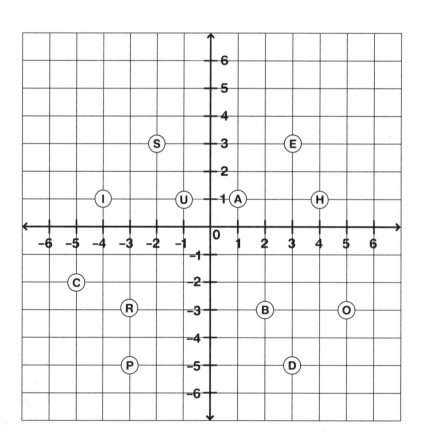

Algebra Readiness Scholastic Professional Books

Scatterplot Scores

Students get the score on their favorite basketball players when they use coordinate graphing to make a scatterplot of sports scores.

⟳→ Directions

1. Distribute one cut-out box score (or copy of a box score) to each pair, along with a piece of graph paper and scratch paper.

2. Students look at the statistics for the team that won the game. On paper, one student writes the number of minutes each athlete played during the game. The other student writes the number of points each athlete scored.

3. On the graph paper, students draw an *x*-axis and a *y*-axis. They label the *x*-axis "Minutes Played" and the *y*-axis "Points Scored."

4. The student who wrote the number of minutes each athlete played counts out how many spaces to move to the right on the graph. The student who wrote points scored counts how many spaces to move vertically on the graph.

5. Students mark a point on the graph for each athlete, labeling the point with the athlete's last name.

6. When the graphs are complete, tack them to a bulletin board to share with the class. Ask students who are familiar with basketball to help you analyze the scatterplots in a class discussion. For example, how does a player's team position influence his or her spot on the graph? [Due to their role on the court, defensive players may play for a long time and score few points.]

✩ Taking It Farther

Challenge students to keep track of statistics at school basketball games and make scatterplots from the results. If they make scatterplots from several games, can they see any trends?

✓ Assessing Skills

Observe whether students label the graphs correctly. Are they able to explain what the points marked on the graphs represent?

LEARNING OBJECTIVE

Students use coordinates to make a scatterplot graph.

GROUPING

Pairs

MATERIALS

✳ basketball box scores from the sports section of a newspaper (Activity should be done during basketball season if possible; otherwise, save sports sections of the paper from basketball season.)

✳ graph paper

✳ scratch paper and pencil

Integer Football

Play this fun game and get ready for a kickoff of intensive integer computation practice. Students won't fumble positive and negative numbers again!

Directions

1. Duplicate the *Integer Football* reproducible for each pair. Review the terms *integer*, *positive*, and *negative* with the class.

2. One player takes the side of the Touchdown Negatives, while the other takes the side of the Pigskin Positives. To start, each player's three counters are placed on the 0-yard line. The object is for players to get all three of their counters to their own 50-yard lines (positive or negative) first.

3. Players use a pencil and paper clip to make the spinner, spinning the clip around the pencil.

4. For each turn, a player spins the Yards spinner and moves a counter the number of positive or negative yards indicated. To clarify, draw the following number line on the board:

```
←——————————————————————————————————→
 -50 -40 -30 -20 -10  0  10  20  30  40  50
```

Suppose a player who had a counter on the 10-yard line spins a –30. Draw an arrow as below, or move a counter to show students that the player would move 30 yards to the left.

```
←——————————————————————————————————→
 -50 -40 -30 -20 -10  0  10  20  30  40  50
```

5. If all three of one player's counters land on the opposing side's 50-yard line, all those counters should be moved back to 0. A player does not need an exact spin to land on a 50-yard line. The first player to get all three counters on his or her own 50-yard line wins.

Taking It Farther

To make the game harder, duplicate the reproducible. Change +10 and –10 to +5 and –5, change +20 and –20 to +15 and –15, and change +30 and –30 to +25 and –25. Use a ruler to draw 5-yard lines between the 10-yard lines. Make copies of the new reproducible for students to play the game again.

Assessing Skills

Observe whether students understand which direction to move a counter that is already on the negative side of the board. If they spin a –10, do they move 10 yards to the left? Students may be confused and move to the –10 yard line instead.

LEARNING OBJECTIVE

Students add positive and negative integers.

GROUPING

Pairs

MATERIALS

✳ *Integer Football* reproducible (p. 49)

✳ pencil and paper clip for each pair (to make the spinner)

✳ 3 different-colored counters for each student

Integer Football

Attention sports fans—and math fans! Are you ready to tackle a fun new game?
Your goal is to get all your players to your own team's 50-yard line. Don't fumble!

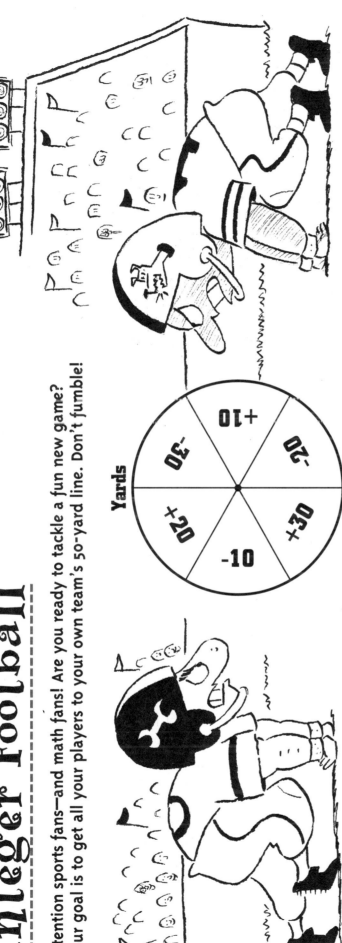

Yards

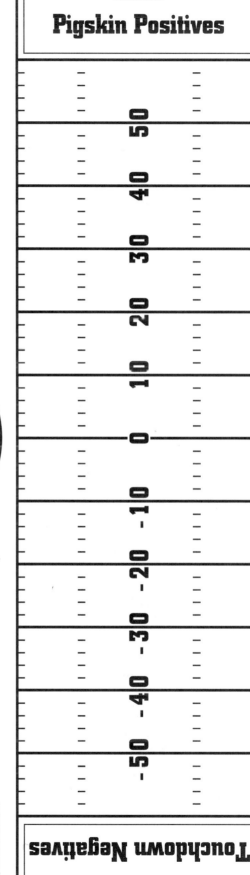

Pigskin Positives

Touchdown Negatives

Mouthwatering Math!

When students use candy manipulatives to add integers, they'll get some sweet computation and problem-solving practice. Algebra never tasted so good!

⟿ Directions

1. Separate the candy by color. Each pair of players gets two candy colors, ten of each. They decide which color will represent positive integers and which will represent negative integers.

2. Each pair arranges their three cups or bowls in a triangle.

3. Player 1 turns his or her back. Meanwhile, Player 2 puts candy in each cup, using only one color in each cup. For example, if yellow is positive and green is negative, three yellow candies represent +3. Five green candies represent –5. (Note: Player 2 does not have to use all the available candy.)

4. Player 2 finds the sum of the integers in two adjacent cups. She or he writes the sum on a piece of paper and places the paper between the two cups. Player 2 does this for each pair of integers so there is a piece of paper between each pair of cups.

5. Player 2 removes the candy from the cups and places it in front of Player 1.

6. Player 1 turns around. Using the candy and the sums on the paper between each pair of cups, Player 1 figures out how many candies— and which color—go in each cup.

7. Players switch roles and play again.

★ Taking It Farther

After a few rounds, have students try the game using subtraction instead of addition. To find the difference to write on the paper between two bowls, players first subtract the left number from the right number, then subtract the right number from the left number. The answers should be the positive and negative versions of an integer, such as ±5.

✔ Assessing Skills

* What strategies do students use? Guess and check may be one method.

* Do they realize that one of the sums on the paper will be the total number of positive or negative candies they are handed (assuming both colors were used)?

LEARNING OBJECTIVE

Students add positive and negative integers.

GROUPING

Pairs

MATERIALS

* large bag of round, colored candy (Different-colored plastic chips or markers can be substituted for candy.)

* 3 bowls or cups for each pair of students

* paper and pencil for each pair

Square Off!

Students get squared away with squares and square roots as they complete a cross-number puzzle.

◉▸ Directions

1. Duplicate the *Square Off!* reproducible for each student.

2. Review the terms *square* (as in square of a number) and *square root*.

3. Write the following numbers on the board:

25	$[5^2, 5]$
49	$[7^2, 7]$
64	$[8^2, 8]$
169	$[13^2, 13]$

   Ask volunteers to identify the square and the square root for each number. Answers are given in brackets.

4. Let students complete the reproducible on their own. If you want, they may use calculators for computation and to check answers.

☆ Taking It Farther

Encourage students to create their own cross-number puzzles. If exponents have been covered in class, students may use exponents greater than 2 in their puzzles. They may also use cube roots. Each student then gives his or her puzzle to a classmate to solve.

✔ Assessing Skills

✳ Do students use multiplication and division to check their answers?

✳ If an answer going down does not fit with an answer going across the same space, what do students do?

LEARNING OBJECTIVE

Students find squares and square roots of numbers.

GROUPING

Individual

MATERIALS

✳ *Square Off!* reproducible (p. 52)

✳ calculators (optional)

ANSWERS

Across	Down
B. 9	**A.** 10
C. 81	**B.** 900
F. 400	**D.** 1,024
H. 289	**G.** 18
I. 324	**H.** 2,601
L. 144	**J.** 22
N. 14	**K.** 441
O. 15	**M.** 25

Square Off!

You're no square! So go ahead—find squares and square roots of numbers to fill in the cross-number puzzle. The answer for Across A is done for you.

A **1**	**6**	■	B	■	C	D
	■	F			■	
■	G			■		
H			■	I	J	
	■		K	■		■
	■	L			■	M
N		■		■	O	

ACROSS

A. 4^2

B. $\sqrt{81}$

C. 9^2

F. 20^2

H. 17^2

I. 18^2

L. 12^2

N. $\sqrt{196}$

O. $\sqrt{225}$

DOWN

A. $\sqrt{100}$

B. 30^2

D. 32^2

G. $\sqrt{324}$

H. 51^2

J. $\sqrt{484}$

K. 21^2

M. $\sqrt{625}$

52

Algebra Readiness Scholastic Professional Books

Laboratory Labyrinth

As students wind their way through this maze to a mad scientist's lab, they find squares and square roots at every turn!

⟶ Directions

1. For each student, duplicate the *Laboratory Labyrinth* reproducible.

2. Review squares and square roots with the class. To complete your review, call on volunteers to write examples of some squares and square roots on the board.

3. Distribute the reproducible. Explain that to find the correct path through the castle, students must follow Maddy Seintyst's directions, located at the top of the maze. For each step, students find the square or square root of the number as indicated. Then they draw a line through the passage that contains the answer.

4. Let students complete the reproducible on their own.

5. When students have finished, allow time for them to compare answers. Was there more than one way to get through the maze?

☆ Taking It Farther

Challenge students to create and illustrate their own mazes. To make the mazes more challenging, you can have them use exponents other than 2 and cube roots in the clues.

✓ Assessing Skills

Note whether students confuse the operations of finding a square and finding a square root. Some students may also multiply a number by 2 instead of finding the square, or divide by 2 when they want to find the square root. In the maze, using the wrong method sometimes leads students down a wrong path.

LEARNING OBJECTIVE

Students calculate squares and square roots.

GROUPING

Individual

MATERIALS

✳ *Laboratory Labyrinth* reproducible (p. 54)

ANSWERS

3

256

100

12

7

1,296

11

8

144

Laboratory Labyrinth

Hi! I'm Maddy Seintyst. I've got to get back to the lab. I think I left a Bunsen burner on! Unfortunately, the passages of my castle are filled with all kinds of danger.

Use squares and square roots to help me follow my map, or I'm a goner!

Directions to the lab.
- $\sqrt{9}$
- 16^2
- 10^2
- $\sqrt{144}$
- $\sqrt{49}$
- 36^2
- $\sqrt{121}$
- $\sqrt{64}$
- 12^2

Paper Patterns

Students will "half" a great time figuring out the pattern that evolves when a piece of paper is folded again and again.

LEARNING OBJECTIVE

Students make a table to find a pattern.

GROUPING

Pairs

MATERIALS

❊ paper and pencil

◉➔ Directions

1. Start by discussing patterns. Tell students that to complete a pattern, they can decide what math was done to get each successive number in the pattern. Then they can test the idea to make sure it works.

2. Hold up a piece of paper and fold it in half, like this:

   Have each pair of students fold a piece of paper as well. Note to the class that with 1 fold, you have 2 sections of paper.

3. Now fold the paper again, like this:

   With 2 folds, there are now 4 sections.

4. On the board, write a table like the following:

PATTERN OF FOLDS

FOLDS	SECTIONS
1	2
2	4

Have students copy and continue the table on their own paper, looking for patterns. After 3 folds, each pair should try to predict how many sections there will be with 6 folds. Then they can test to see if their predictions were correct.

✪ Taking It Farther

A piece of paper can be folded only a few times. But say it could be folded 15, 20, or 25 times. Challenge students to find ways to figure out how many sections there would be. One way is to continue the table, doubling the number of sections each time. Another way is to express FOLDS as *n*, and SECTIONS as 2*n*. So after 15 folds, you'd have 2 × 15, or 30 sections.

✔ Assessing Skills

Observe how many folds it takes for students to discover the pattern. Are they able to correctly predict how many sections there will be after 6 folds?

Function Detective

Students use math clues to get hot on the trail of a mystery function!

⟳→ Directions

1. Review the term *function* with students.

2. Divide the class into groups of four students. Two students in each group should work together to write a simple function, such as $f(x) = 3x + 2$ on an index card. The other two students are the Function Detectives who figure out the function.

3. The Function Detectives turn their backs so they cannot see the function. The Function Detectives then write a number on a separate index card and hand it to the students who hold the function.

4. The students plug the number into the function and write the answer on the Function Detectives' card. For example, if the function is $f(x) = 3x - 2$, and the card reads 3, the students write $3 \rightarrow 7$ on the card. Then they hand it back to the Function Detectives.

5. The Function Detectives write another number on another card and repeat the process. After the Function Detectives have collected several cards, they try to guess what the function is.

6. When the Function Detectives have figured out the function, students switch roles. The former Function Detectives write a function. The other pair of students are now the Function Detectives.

★ Taking It Farther

As they play more rounds of the game, challenge students to find the functions with fewer and fewer tries.

✓ Assessing Skills

Have each student write a journal entry describing the strategies he or she used to find the functions.

LEARNING OBJECTIVE

Students find the functions that describe number patterns.

GROUPING

Cooperative groups of 4

MATERIALS

✳ several index cards or pieces of paper for each student

Crunchy Functions

Watch students sink their teeth into functions and problem solving (not to mention snack crackers) with this tasty hands-on activity!

⟶ Directions

1. Review the terms *function* and *perimeter* with students. Explain to groups that they will use crackers to find functions in shape patterns.

2. FUNCTION 1: On the board, draw one square. Note that if you call each side 1 unit, the square has a perimeter of 4 units.

3. Draw another square next to and touching to the first one. Ask students: *What is the perimeter now?* [6 units]

4. Next, have each group place crackers in a row to discover the perimeter for a row of 3, 4, 5, 6, or 7 crackers. Have them determine what function can be used to figure the perimeter for a row of 15 squares. [If *s* = the number of squares, the function is $2s + 2$. So a row of 15 squares has a perimeter of 32.]

5. FUNCTION 2: Tell students that in this activity, they will be building large squares from the small cracker squares. Draw squares on the board as shown. Point out that to make a square with a length of 1 unit, you need 1 cracker. To make a square with a length of 2 units, you need 4 crackers.

6. Have students use crackers to make squares with lengths of 3, 4, and 5 units. Let them determine how many crackers it will take. Ask: *What function could be used to find the number of crackers you would need to make a square with a length of 12 units?* [If ℓ = the length of the square, the function is $\ell \times \ell$, or ℓ^2. So for a 12-unit-long square, you need 144 crackers.]

7. FUNCTION 3: Have students build squares to find the function for the perimeter. Ask: *What is the perimeter of a square with a length of 12 units?* [Where ℓ = length, the perimeter is 4ℓ. For the 12-unit square, the perimeter is 48 units.]

☆ Taking It Farther

Let students use sugar cubes to find functions for the surface area of a stack of cubes, and for large cubes made out of smaller cubes.

✓ Assessing Skills

Observe whether students test their functions to see if they work.

Missing Museums

Students find the missing number that completes each pattern and learn where some of the wildest and wackiest museums are located!

⟳→ Directions

1. Duplicate the *Missing Museums* reproducible for each student.

2. Discuss number patterns with the class. Ask students: *What is the difference between a pattern and a group of random numbers?*

3. Talk about how students can find the missing number in a pattern. One way is to hypothesize about what was done to each number in order to reach the next number in the pattern. Then test the theory to see if it works.

4. Write the following examples on the board:
   2, 5, 8, 11, 14, ...
   2, 5, 11, 23, 47, ...

   Ask volunteers to find the number that comes next in each pattern and explain how they found the answer. [In the first example, 3 is added to each succeeding number, so the next number in the pattern is 17. In the second example, each number is multiplied by 2, and 1 is added to the product. So the next number in the pattern is 95.]

5. Note that in the examples, the first two numbers are the same. Can students think of any other ways to complete a pattern that begins with 2, 5, ... ? [One possible answer: Take each number squared and then add 1. So the pattern would be: 2, 5, 26, 677, and so on. Another possible answer: Multiply each number by 3 and subtract 1. So the pattern would be: 2, 5, 14, 41, 122, and so on.]

6. Distribute the reproducible and let students complete it on their own.

★ Taking It Farther

Have students write journal entries explaining the strategies and tests they used to discover the number patterns in the activity. Challenge each student to come up with a number pattern for the rest of the class to solve. Can students find more than one way to complete some of the patterns?

✓ Assessing Skills

Ask students to explain verbally the reasoning behind their answers to the problems on the reproducible. Ask: *What numbers would continue the sequences even further?*

LEARNING OBJECTIVE

Students complete number patterns.

GROUPING

Individual

MATERIALS

✳ *Missing Museums* reproducible (p. 59)

✳ pencils

✳ scrap paper

ANSWERS

A. 14

B. 63

C. 129

D. 20

E. 27

F. 34 (Fibonacci sequence)

G. 12

H. 19 (prime numbers)

Missing Museums

Meet Anne DeSplay. She just loves museums! Anne was planning a trip to see some of her favorite museums in the U.S., but she got them all mixed up. Now, Anne needs your help!

To find out where each real museum is located, figure out what number completes each number pattern in the left column. Draw a line to your answer in the right column.

MUSEUM NAMES

A. Tupperware Historic Food Container Museum
224, 112, 56, 28,...

B. Museum of Bad Art
11, 24, 37, 50,...

C. Hall of Flame (Fire Fighting Museum)
5, 9, 17, 33, 65,...

D. Leroy's Motorcycle Museum
2, 5, 0, 0, 8, 11, 0, 0, 14, 17, 0, 0,...

E. National Museum of Roller Skating
48, 47, 45, 42, 38, 33,...

F. Tolbert's Chili Parlor and Museum of Chili
1, 1, 2, 3, 5, 8, 13, 21,...

G. The Potato Museum
60.75, 40.5, 27, 18,...

H. The Museum of Pez (candy) Memorabilia
2, 3, 5, 7, 11, 13, 17,...

MUSEUM LOCATIONS

27 Lincoln, Nebraska

19 Burlingame, California

63 Boston, Massachusetts

14 Orlando, Florida

34 Dallas, Texas

12 Albuquerque, New Mexico

20 Wichita, Kansas

129 Phoenix, Arizona

Do I Have Problems!

Use these quick skill builders as a class warm-up, for students who finish tests early, or just for a fun break from the textbook!

STORMY WEATHER

How do meteorologists predict how long a thunderstorm will last? One way they find an estimate is by using the following formula:

$$t^2 = \frac{d^3}{216}$$

In this formula, t = the length of time the storm will last (in hours), and d = the diameter of the storm. If the diameter of a storm is 6 miles, about how long will the storm last? [1 hour]

WE'RE TELLING THE TOOTH!

Bite into variables to find out some amazing facts about teeth! For each problem, plug in these variable values: $t = 4$, $k = 500{,}000$, $m = 72.3$. Write your answer in the blank space to complete the tooth fact.

a. $t^2 \div 2$ The teeth of a Tyrannosaurus rex dinosaur were as long as ____ inches! [8]

b. $80k$ About _____ Americans never go to a dentist. [40,000,000]

c. $32m - 2{,}213.6$ Crocodiles have up to ____ teeth. [100]

d. $1{,}500{,}008 - 3k$ One out of every ____ people has no teeth. [8]

AGE-OLD PROBLEM

Right now, Jamal's mother is 3 times older than Jamal. But in 12 years, her age will be exactly 2 times greater than Jamal's. How old are Jamal and his mother today? [Jamal is 12. His mother is 36.]

HEADS UP

Rachel's uncle Rupert invited her to visit his llama and ostrich farm. Today he asked her to help out by counting all the llamas and ostriches in the barn. The animals are running around so fast, Rachel just can't keep track. But she's sure she counted 35 heads and 94 feet. How many llamas are there? How many ostriches are there? (Remember: Llamas have 4 feet; ostriches are birds that have 2 feet.) [23 ostriches, 12 llamas]

SWEET DIVISION

Larissa has a bag full of gumdrops. She knows there are fewer than 75 pieces of candy in all. When she divides them into groups of 3, 4, 5, or 6, there is always 1 gumdrop left over. How many gumdrops does Larissa have? [61 gumdrops]

PICTURE THIS!

On a piece of graph paper, draw an *x*- and a *y*-axis. Make sure you leave room to move 33 spaces to the right on the *x*-axis and 18 spaces up on the *y*-axis.

Begin marking off the following points. As you mark each point, draw a line to connect it to the previous point. When you're done, the connected dots will make a picture. What is it? [picture of a shark]

a. (4, 4)
b. (7, 3)
c. (16, 2)
d. (25, 3)
e. (29, 5)
f. (32, 2)

g. (31, 6)
h. (33, 12)
i. (29, 8)
j. (25, 10)
k. (19, 12)
l. (18, 18)

m. (11, 12)
n. (4, 10)
o. (0, 8)
p. (3, 5)
q. (6, 5)
r. (4, 4)

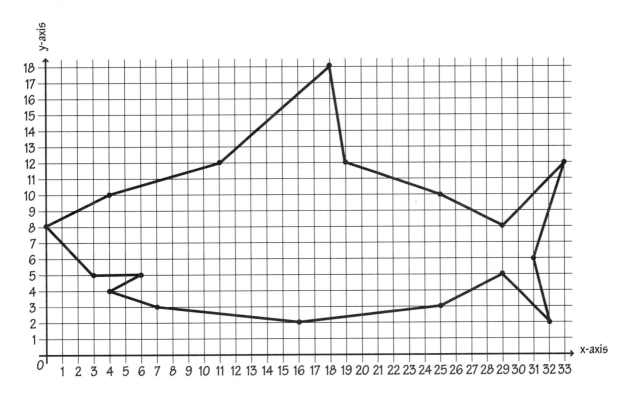

61

Name _____ Date _____

In My Opinion

The activity _____ was:
(name of activity)

Easy   Hard

because:

_____

_____

_____

_____

My work on this activity was:

poor   fair   good   excellent

because:

_____

_____

_____

I used the following math strategy or strategies:

➔ _____   ➔ _____

➔ _____   ➔ _____

➔ _____   ➔ _____

I would share this tip with someone who is about to do this activity:

_____

_____

Activity ———————— Date —————

TEACHER ASSESSMENT FORM

Student					
UNDERSTANDING					
Identifies the problem or task.					
Understands the math concept.					
SOLVING					
Develops and carries out a plan.					
Uses strategies, models, and tools effectively.					
DECIDING					
Is able to convey reasoning behind decision making.					
Understands why approach did or didn't work.					
LEARNING					
Comments on solution.					
Connects solution to other math or real-world applications.					
Makes general rule about solution or extends it to a more complicated problem.					
COMMUNICATING					
Understands and uses mathematical language effectively.					
COLLABORATING					
Participates by sharing ideas with partner or group members.					
Listens to partner or other group members.					
ACCOMPLISHING					
Shows progress in problem solving.					
Undertakes difficult tasks and perseveres in solving them.					
Is confident of mathematical abilities.					

SCORING RUBRIC

3	2	1
Fully accomplishes the task.	Partially accomplishes the task.	Does not accomplish the task.
Shows full understanding of key mathematical idea(s).	Shows partial understanding of key mathematical idea(s).	Shows little or no grasp of key mathematical idea(s).
Communicates thinking clearly using oral explanation or written, symbolic, or visual means.	Oral or written explanation partially communicates thinking but may be incomplete, misdirected, or not clearly presented.	Recorded work or oral explanation is fragmented and not understandable.

Notes